GATESHEAD
THEN & NOW
IN COLOUR

ROB KIRKUP

The
History
Press

First published in 2015

The History Press
The Mill, Brimscombe Port
Stroud, Gloucestershire, GL5 2QG
www.thehistorypress.co.uk

British Library Cataloguing in Publication Data.
A catalogue record for this book is available from the British Library.

ISBN 978 0 7524 6567 8

Typesetting and origination by The History Press
Printed in India.

CONTENTS

Acknowledgements   4

About the Author   4

Introduction   5

Gateshead Then & Now   6

ACKNOWLEDGEMENTS

I would like to thank my friends and family for all their support and words of encouragement while compiling *Gateshead Then & Now*.

Archive images were provided by Gateshead Libraries except where otherwise stated. All present-day images were taken by the author with an Olympus PEN E-PL1 camera.

ABOUT THE AUTHOR

ROB KIRKUP is a local and paranormal historian and the author of a number of regional titles, including *Wallsend Then & Now*, *Newcastle Then & Now* and *Ghostly Tyne & Wear*. He lives in Wallsend, Tyne & Wear.

INTRODUCTION

The novelist and playwright J.B. Priestley wrote of Gateshead in his best-selling 1934 travelogue *English Journey*: 'If there is any town of like size on the continent of Europe that can show a similar lack of civic dignity and all the evidence of urban civilization, I should like to know its name and quality. No true civilization could have produced such a town, which is nothing better than a huge dingy dormitory.' He added, 'The whole town appeared to have been carefully planned by an enemy of the human race. Insects can do better than this.'

This impression has proven typical of how Gateshead has been viewed by those who do not call the town home. Much, however, has changed and the Gateshead of today bears little resemblance to that outdated view.

The first recorded mention of Gateshead is in the writings of the Venerable Bede who referred to an abbot of Gateshead called Utta in 623. However, a settlement has existed on the Gateshead side of the River Tyne since at least Roman times, located next to the only bridge over the river, now the site of the current Swing Bridge.

In 1068, William the Conqueror defeated the forces of Edgar the Ætheling (heir to the throne of England) and Malcolm King of Scotland at Gateshead Fell (now Low Fell and Sheriff Hill).

Gateshead was under the jurisdiction of the Bishop of Durham during medieval times. At this time the area was largely forest, and the forest was the subject of Gateshead's first charter when, in approximately 1164, rules were set down for the use of the forest by the people of the town.

In 1835, Gateshead was established as a municipal borough within County Durham. This was to change following the Local Government Act of 1972, and in 1974 Tyne and Wear was formed; a metropolitan county made up of the boroughs of North Tyneside, South Tyneside, the City of Sunderland, the City of Newcastle, and Gateshead.

In recent years, Gateshead Council has set their sights on making Gateshead a city, and plans are underway to develop the town. The most notable transformation thus far has occurred on the Quayside, with Millennium Bridge, Sage Gateshead, and the Baltic Centre for Contemporary Art all being constructed since the dawn of the twenty-first century.

One famous Gateshead landmark, which encapsulated the opinion of those who considered Gateshead to be an ugly, industrial town, was the Trinity Centre car park. Dominating the town centre for many years, it gained an iconic status by featuring prominently in the 1971 movie *Get Carter*, starring Michael Caine. Despite fierce public opposition, it was demolished in 2010 and replaced with the £150 million Trinity Square shopping complex.

Gateshead is also home to Antony Gormley's Angel of the North, one of Britain's largest sculptures. Erected in 1998, it has already become synonymous worldwide with Gateshead.

Gateshead is the home of the Metrocentre, the largest shopping centre in the European Union, and the Team Valley Trading Estate, still one of the largest purpose-built commercial estates in the UK.

This book chronicles the transformation of Gateshead by showing how forty-five of the town's landmarks have changed over the years.

Rob Kirkup, 2015

No. 19 West Street

THIS PHOTOGRAPH, TAKEN in the late nineteenth century, shows a large family home in Mirk Place, close to Gateshead's Quayside. This was the home in which celebrated engraver Thomas Bewick lived and died. Thomas had worked his entire life in Newcastle upon Tyne as a general engraver on metal and copperplate, at the same time earning the reputation for being the father of modern wood engraving. Thomas never

stopped working completely, although he semi-retired with his wife Isabella and their children to Gateshead, where they bought this house in 1812.

Despite being in the heart of the town, there were very few buildings around the Bewick family home, and he could see as far as the steeple of Holy Cross church at Ryton, 8 miles away.

Thomas died in the house on 8 November 1828, the same year that his wife also passed away. They were succeeded by their children, who continued to live in the Bewick family home. Jane Bewick, their eldest daughter, dedicated her life to the veneration of her father's memory, including the publication of her father's memoirs in 1862; *A Memoir of Thomas Bewick, written by himself. Embellished by numerous wood engravings, designed and engraved by the author for a work on British fishes, and never before published*, written by Thomas himself, at the request of Jane, in the final years of his life.

Jane passed away in 1881. In the following year her younger sister, Isabella, carried out Jane's wishes to give the British Museum a substantial collection of watercolours and woodcuts by their father, some of which had been exhibited in London in November and December 1880. Isabella passed away in 1883; both sisters died in the family home.

By 1897 the building had been demolished, as had all of Mirk Place, to make way for the current West Street. Upon the site of the Bewick home, No. 19 West Street was built as a post office.

THE IMPORTANCE OF Thomas Bewick in Gateshead's history has not been overlooked, however, as the nearby Bewick Road was named for him, and today a plaque adorns the wall of the listed red-brick building which reads: 'Upon the site of this building stood the house wherein lived and died Thomas Bewick the wood engraver. Born 1753. Died 1828.'

The building has long since closed as a post office and is now Workplace Gallery: a contemporary art gallery.

AMEN CORNER

AMEN CORNER, OR the Holy Corner as it was also known, was the junction where
Belle Vue Terrace, Durham Road, Gladstone Terrace, and High West Street met, and
a place where three churches stood. Captured here, the first building on the left of
the photograph is the Baptist church, the building beyond it (with the spire) is the
Presbyterian church, and across the road on the right of the photograph is the United
Free Methodist church. The railings in the foreground on the right are the railings of the
Abbott Memorial School.

From 1882 the Methodist church was
no longer a place of worship, instead it was
used as a hall of varieties, a boxing hall,
a Salvation Army hall and, in 1887, it was
opened as the Theatre Royal. It was in this
building, on 26 December 1891, that nine
young children and an adult tragically lost
their lives during a fire alarm at a pantomime
performance of *Aladdin*. One boy dropped
a penny and then set fire to a programme
with a match to give himself enough light
to find it. The alarm was sounded and the
ten victims were crushed to death as people
panicked and tried to get out of the building.
Only two buckets of water were needed to put
out the small fire.

IN THE 1950S, most of the buildings in
the original photograph were pulled down,
and the land was cleared for the building of
the Gateshead Highway. The only church that
survives is Durham Road Baptist church; it
has served the Baptists of the town since it
was built in 1877.

ANGEL OF THE NORTH

MADE OF 200 tonnes of steel and standing 65ft high, with a 175ft wingspan, the *Angel of the North* dominates the skyline for miles around.

It is seen here on 20 June 1998, at the official unveiling of the much-talked-about sculpture. Gateshead Council hosted 'Celebrating an Angel' day, a free event including entertainment by musicians and artists, an opportunity to see angel artwork by local children, and an auction of the No. 9 Newcastle United football shirt in which the *Angel* had been draped amid much publicity. There was even the chance to meet the man behind the design of the *Angel of the North*: Antony Gormley.

Upon its conception, the *Angel of the North* generated much controversy in the media, with the British press running many negative news articles, including a 'Gateshead Stop the Statue' campaign. Local councillors and public figures were also very vocal in their opposition to the sculpture.

TODAY, DESPITE ITS lonely position on a hilltop overlooking the A1 on the southern edge of Low Fell, the *Angel of the North* is visited by over 150,000 people each year, and is seen by more than 90,000 drivers each day passing along the A1.

Despite the original opposition to the sculpture, it has become a local landmark, often used to represent Tyneside alongside the Tyne Bridge and the Millennium Bridge, and the people of Gateshead are proud of 'their' *Angel of the North*. In 2006 it was even chosen as part of a government-sponsored Culture Online project as one of twelve official 'Icons of England' alongside others such as Stonehenge, the FA Cup, and the Routemaster double-decker bus.

AXWELL HALL

IN 1629, MAYOR of Newcastle and merchant adventurer Sir James Clavering, 1st Baronet, purchased the Axwell Park estate, which included a manor house. His descendant, Sir Thomas Clavering, 7th Baronet, demolished the existing manor house in 1758 and had a substantial mansion built in its place to the Palladian designs of James Paine, one of England's most notable architects of the period. This mansion would be called Axwell Hall, and would be the seat of the family until the 10th and final baronet, Sir Henry Augustus Clavering, passed away in 1893 with no heirs.

Axwell Hall's usage is unclear in the years between 1893 and 1922. In 1922 it became an industrial school, before changing to an approved school in 1933 – an institution similar to a boarding school, except that the young people who attend were made to go there by a court, either because they had committed criminal offences or because they were beyond parental control.

In 1933 there were 150 'inmates' – boys from Newcastle, Sunderland, Middlesbrough, Durham, Yorkshire and Northumberland.

The school was closed in 1981, and the hall and the majority of the 35-acre grounds of Axwell Park were sold.

LEFT EMPTY AND neglected, the Grade II listed building (situated just east of Blaydon) began to deteriorate, that was until 2006 when property developers bought the hall and the estate to restore and convert it into luxury apartments. This photograph was taken in the summer of 2014, during this period of restoration. The project is on schedule to be completed in 2016, when the resulting twenty apartments will be put up for sale.

BALTIC CENTRE FOR CONTEMPORARY ART

THE BALTIC FLOUR Mill was designed by Hull-based architects Gelder and Kitchen for Rank Hovis in the late 1930s to be built on the south bank of the River Tyne, on the former site of the Gateshead Ironworks; famous for their work on the High Level Bridge that spans the Tyne. The foundations went up, but the outbreak of the Second World War led to the project being halted. Work resumed on the mill in 1948, and it was finally completed in 1950. Even though it was built to the 1930s designs, it was equipped with the most modern machinery of the time; it had a silo capacity of 22,000 tonnes and could despatch 240 tonnes of grain per hour.

It was one of a number of mills located along the banks of the Tyne, all of which, due to their size, became prominent local landmarks.

At its height around 300 people were employed at the Baltic Flour Mill, with some of them moving to the area specifically to work there. In 1957 an animal food mill extension was built and the Baltic became a dual-purpose mill: producing animal feed as well as grain.

In 1981, after only a little over thirty years in operation and with the number of people employed at the mill down to around 100, the Baltic Flour Mill ceased production.

The building remained unused and derelict for some time and the future of the industrial landmark looked uncertain. This was to change in 1992 when plans were drawn up to convert the building into an international centre for contemporary visual art. An architectural design competition was launched by Gateshead Council and the Royal Institute of British Architects, and in 1994, Dominic Williams of Ellis Williams Architects, London was announced as the winner. This photograph was taken in 1996, two years before work began on the £50 million project, which included £33.4 million from the Arts Council Lottery Fund.

ONLY THE SOUTH and north walls, and the four brick corner towers of the original 1950s building remain today. Its completely new interior consisted of six main floors and three mezzanines, offering 3,000sq.m of arts space, artists' studios, cinema/lecture space, shop, a library and archive for the study of contemporary art. This is topped off by a glass rooftop restaurant offering stunning panoramic views of Gateshead, Newcastle and beyond.

The Baltic Centre for Contemporary Art opened to the public at midnight on Saturday, 13 July 2002, and the inaugural exhibition, B.OPEN, attracted over 35,000 visitors in the first week. The Baltic has proved a huge success, with over 5 million visitors passing through its doors to date. Along with the Millennium Bridge and the Sage Gateshead, the Baltic has helped to transform Gateshead's Quayside.

BILL QUAY

BILL QUAY IS a village on the south bank of the River Tyne, situated between Pelaw to the west and Hebburn to the east.

During the nineteenth century, Bill Quay was an area of industry. In 1818 the first shipyard was set up there by William Boutland and this – along with another yard which had been set up by Robert and John Maddison – would go on to become R.B. Harrison's Ship Repair Yard. Other industries included coke manufacture and the chemical industry, with four chemical works.

Also established in 1818 was the paintworks of Hoyle, Robson and Barnett, when Richard Hoyle took over the building which had been a colour works since at least 1787. It can be seen here in this photograph of the Bill Quay waterfront in 1898 and is the large building in the centre. The wording along the frontage reads 'Hoyle, Robson and Barnett Ltd. Manufacturer of Paints, Dry Colours, Varnishes etc. Established 1818.' In 1856, Barnett had become the principle shareholder. R.B. Harrison's shipyard can also be seen in this photograph to the left of the paintworks. Bill Quay's terraces can be seen behind the waterfront industrial buildings.

THE PRESENT-DAY photograph, taken from the Walker Riverside on the opposite side of the Tyne, shows that most of the industrial buildings from the late nineteenth-century image remain, although Harrison's shipyard is nothing more than a ruined shell with no roof, and the paintworks is also empty, unused, with virtually all of the windows boarding up or smashed. The most successful industry on the waterfront now is the car salvage yard. The hills beyond the former factories are nicely landscaped and a lot of the housing from the original photograph has long since been demolished.

BIRTLEY
CO-OPERATIVE STORE

IT WAS IN 1861 that the Birtley Co-operative Society was formed. The first co-operative societies appeared in the nineteenth century, spreading throughout Britain and France. As the 'Co-op' appeared in more and more towns and villages, it became the most important store for locals as those using it would become members of the Co-operative Society and would be paid a dividend.

The Birtley Co-operative Society's first premises were in Mount Pleasant, before moving to Durham Road, and then to a much larger location at Harras Bank. On Christmas Day 1900, disaster struck when fire broke out in the store and ravaged the building completely.

Rather than rebuild the Harras Bank store, the Co-op moved to a new permanent store on Durham Road. It is pictured here in around 1920.

TODAY THE IMPORTANCE of the Co-operative Society has diminished as supermarket chains have extended and are the first port of call for most people when grocery shopping. The Co-operative market share of food retail peaked at 30 per cent in the 1950s, and is now around 6 per cent.

Older residents of the village will no doubt remember their parents having to give their dividend number on every visit to the store. Birtley still has a Co-operative presence in the form of a popular Co-op food store, a travel agent and a funeral parlour. Co-operative Food Supply Chain Logistics is a distribution business and the head office is in Birtley.

The former premises on Durham Road, pictured here in 2014, now houses a number of smaller shops including a local Cancer support charity shop, Birtley Bed Centre, Ladbrokes bookmakers, and a sandwich shop.

The traffic cones that can be seen on the opposite side of the road form a temporary walkway for pedestrians as a new Morrisons supermarket is being built.

BLACK'S REGAL CINEMA

THE BLACK'S REGAL at No. 306 High Street was built
in 1936–37. The newest cinema in Gateshead was also
the most lavish, with a magnificent Compton organ that
would be played during performances.

On 15 February 1937, the mayor, Alderman White,
officiated at the grand opening and the cinema was
officially opened by actress Gracie Fields. Gracie was
a megastar of the day; she was the highest paid
film and music star in the nation, but interrupted a
holiday in St Moritz to travel to Gateshead to open the
Black's Regal Cinema. She performed from the roof
of the cinema to crowds of thousands in the street
below. Traffic came to a complete standstill as people
gathered to watch.

In 1944 the cinema was taken over by the Odeon
chain and the following year it was renamed the
Gateshead Odeon.

By the 1960s the popularity of bingo and television
meant that times were tough for the cinemas.
The Odeon struggled on but, on 18 January 1975,
it was forced to close.

It is pictured here in 1977 by which time it was empty. The following year it reopened as a Top Rank Bingo Club. The bingo hall closed in 1995 and in 2003 the building was demolished.

PROPOSALS WERE MADE to Gateshead Council in 2008 by a property development company to build a hotel, casino and apartment block on this site, but the suggestion of a casino meant that this was declined. Amended proposals were resubmitted by the company in 2011 to construct a six-storey hotel with ninety-seven bedrooms, a bar and restaurant, a retail unit, and a five-storey care home with seventy-two bedrooms. As can be seen here in this modern photograph, these plans have yet to come to fruition, as the former site of the Black's Regal is currently an unused, overgrown piece of landscaped land just south of the William IV public house on the western side of High Street.

BOTTLE BANK

BOTTLE BANK, PICTURED here in 1925, was named for the old Saxon word '*botl*', meaning settlement, and this steeply sloped street was at the heart of old Gateshead. In the eighteenth and early nineteenth centuries, housing and local industry centred around the steep gradient of Bottle Bank and Bridge Street as they led up from the River Tyne, at the point of the only crossing of the river, at the site of the current Swing Bridge. In *Whitehead's Newcastle Directory* for the years 1782–84 (which were the first in which Gateshead was included) there were 145 listed tradesmen, and no less than sixty-five of those were situated in Bottle Bank.

The importance of Bottle Bank declined in the early nineteenth century when Church Street was built, as it offered a gentler gradient, and when the High Level Bridge opened in 1849, Wellington Street became the main route into Gateshead with its bus and railway stations.

During the 1920s much of Bottle Bank was demolished to clear land for the building of the new Tyne Bridge, which opened in 1928, and more buildings were pulled down as part of the 1932–35 slum housing clearance. Over the decades that followed the rest of the former homes, businesses and public houses were destroyed. In 2001, with the rejuvenation of Gateshead's Quayside taking shape in the form of the opening of the Millennium Bridge and plans for the Baltic Centre for Contemporary Art and the Sage Gateshead firmly in place, the last remaining buildings on Bottle Bank were demolished to make way for the building of a new Hilton hotel.

THE MODERN PHOTOGRAPH of Bottle Bank taken in the summertime is barely
recognisable from the photograph taken almost ninety years earlier. The Hilton hotel
can be seen and is hugely popular, offering unrivalled views across the River Tyne.
A statue on the opposite side of the road, which can just be seen beyond the 'Welcome to
Gateshead Quays' sign is the only reminder on the modern-day Bottle Bank of the street's
heritage. Created by North Yorkshire sculptor Peter Coates in 2006, the sculpture bears
the inscription: 'James Hill of Bottle Bank, world renowned fiddle player and composer
of tunes. The finest exponent of the Newcastle hornpipe style. Most active 1842–52.'
James Hill is considered to be one of the most talented fiddler players and tune writers of
the nineteenth century. He is believed to have been born in Scotland in 1811, and from
the 1830s he lived on Bottle Bank near the Hawk Pub with his wife Sarah, who was
born in County Durham. James remained here for most of his life, composing fiddle tunes
that were often named after local pubs and events in the Newcastle and Gateshead areas.
He wrote the tune 'High Level Hornpipe' for the opening of the High Level Bridge.

GATESHEAD
CENTRAL LIBRARY

THE FIRST LIBRARY to be built in Gateshead opened in January 1885 in Swinburne Street. It was built in the 'Romanesque' style of architecture, with a carved head of Archimedes over the front porch. In the first year, over 100,000 books were issued, and the popularity of book loans continued to increase year on year until the outbreak of the First World War.

Following the end of the war the library grew in popularity once more and it became clear that one library could not serve all of Gateshead.

To build a much larger library, a site on Prince Consort Road was bought. This was seen as the perfect site due to its position in a residential area. Newcastle architect

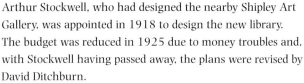

Arthur Stockwell, who had designed the nearby Shipley Art Gallery, was appointed in 1918 to design the new library. The budget was reduced in 1925 due to money troubles and, with Stockwell having passed away, the plans were revised by David Ditchburn.

On 6 April 1926, the present library, pictured here, was opened. The original library was kept open for a number of years as a reading room for 'poor children'. The new library on Prince Consort Road led to the number of library members doubling and book loans increasing by over 33 per cent.

In 1975/76 the building was extended in red brick by borough architect Leslie Berry.

PICTURED HERE IN the modern day, it remains the main library for the town, although it is now one of sixteen to serve Gateshead. The building does not appear to have changed much, but what cannot be seen in this photograph is the £2.6 million refurbishment undertaken in 2010. With funding from the Big Lottery Fund and Gateshead Council, the refurbishment created a new main entrance from the car park. This would also see the library offer a brand new children's library, cafe, young people's space, gallery and a number of community rooms.

CHOPWELL WOODS

CHOPWELL WOODS FIRST formed around 6,000 years ago. This extensive wildwood, comprised mainly of oak and hazel trees, originally covered an area from south of the River Tyne to Allenheads.

From the twelfth century the woods formed part of an estate owned by the Church, but following the Dissolution of the Monasteries, ownership passed to the Crown. By the sixteenth century, Chopwell Woods was being depleted at a rapid rate as timber was taken to repair bridges and castles across the North East, especially in Northumberland and Durham. In 1635, 1,000 trees were felled to construct a warship, *Sovereign of the Seas*, the first ever three-decked warship.

The timber industry continued at Chopwell Woods and was joined by the mining industry in the nineteenth century as the wood was drift undermined for coal. This continued until the early twentieth century.

This image, from around 1903, captures East Carr House, which had formerly been part of the old West Chopwell Farm on the west side of the woods. The family who lived there, and can be seen here, are the Hunter family: William Hunter and his wife and daughter. Sadly, William hanged himself in an outbuilding in 1903. The building collapsed in the early 1930s and by 1935 it was nothing more than a pile of rubble. This pile has reduced over the centuries as locals have taken the stone for other uses such as rockeries.

The turning point for Chopwell Woods came in 1919 when the Forestry Commission took over the management of the wood and, following the Transfer of the Woods Act in 1923, began a full-scale replanting programme.

The Second World War left a permanent scar on Chopwell Woods when three high-explosive bombs fell into the wood, creating three enormous craters.

In 2005, Chopwell Woods was designated under the Plantation on an Ancient Woodland Site (PAWS) scheme, which ensures that only trees native to the area are planted.

TODAY CHOPWELL WOODLAND Park is a real wilderness, with 360 hectares of woodland on the very fringe of Gateshead enjoyed by walkers and cyclists. Miles and miles of paths and tracks allow exploration of this ancient forest from the main car park right into the heart of the wood.

This modern photograph shows one of the many sculptures throughout the park: *The Hands* made of Chopwell poplar in 1994 by local sculptor David Gross.

The long industrial past of timber and coal mining is reflected in the names of the trails and the sculptures to be found within the wood. There's rich, diverse wildlife just waiting to be discovered, including otters, badgers, deer and bats. Even the three craters left by the bombing of the Second World War have become fantastic wildlife habitats themselves, having long since filled with water. There's also a 'Bird of Prey' vantage point where you may be lucky enough to see red kite soaring over the magnificent backdrop of the Derwent Valley beyond. The red kite had been absent from the region for over a century before being reintroduced into the area with great success in 2004.

THE CHURCH OF
ST MARY, HEWORTH

ON WEDNESDAY, 23 MAY 1821, the foundation stone of St Mary's church at Heworth was laid. It replaced a chapel built in 1711, which had become so structurally unsafe that the congregation started to avoid church services there.

An architect had been appointed, but the vicar did most of the design himself to try and save money where possible. On 5 May 1822, the new church was used for the first time by the people of Heworth. Altogether it had cost £2,026 3s 4d and it was a simple sandstone building. The church seated 1,400, and many of these pews were numbered and rented to the wealthier families.

On 6 August the new church was consecrated by the Bishop of Oxford; it was an important day for the village and crowds of people came. All 1,400 seats in the church were full but there was no choir or organ to lead the singing so a professional singer and a cellist were hired.

The church is pictured here in 1924, two years after its centenary, and what cannot be seen in this sepia image is that a century of industrial pollution had coated the church's walls and turned them black. Tramlines can be seen running past the church.

The church has since survived many changes to the village of Heworth. By 1950 the village had begun to disappear, and when the A184 Felling Bypass was built, it sliced not only through Heworth but also through the churchyard.

The building of the Heworth Metro Station in 1975 saw St Mary's church on an island surrounded by traffic. In 1980, plans were drawn up to extend the metro system to Washington; however, this would require the church being demolished as the plans had the new metro lines going right through where the church stood. Fierce opposition came from the parishioners and these plans thankfully never came to pass.

THE PRESENT-DAY photograph shows how little St Mary's church has changed, not only when compared to the 1924 image, but since it first opened its doors. It was cleaned for its 150th birthday back in 1972, returning the exterior walls to their original colour.

CHURCH WALK

CHURCH WALK IS situated along the north wall of St Mary's churchyard, overlooking the River Tyne. This photograph was taken in the 1920s and shows houses on the north side of the street. Built into the steep bankside, these houses enjoyed views of the churchyard

from the front, and a view of the river and Newcastle beyond from the rear. These houses were four- and five-storey tenements housing multiple families, and were amongst some of the worst housing in Gateshead.

The Housing Act of 1930 gave the council much greater power when dealing with slum housing, and between 1932 and 1935 many of the houses on the High Street and the Quayside – including the homes seen here on Church Walk – were acquired by purchase order and demolished.

THE WALK IN the 1920s image will have led to Abbot's Engineering Works but, as can be seen in this photograph taken almost a century later, Church Walk now leads to the west entrance of the Sage Gateshead.

Church Walk is popular with locals and visitors to the area alike for the stunning view it offers across the River Tyne to Newcastle, the Tyne Bridge and the Millennium Bridge below.

31

DUNSTON FLOUR MILL

IN 1887, WORK commenced on the Co-operative Wholesale Society's first major manufacturing works outside of Manchester, in the shape of a huge flour mill at Dunston on the River Tyne.

   When the mill opened on 18 April 1891, it was the largest and most prominent building in Dunston. It was one of the first reinforced-concrete buildings and electric lighting was used throughout the buildings, which included a warehouse, screen-rooms,

a blacksmith's shop and sack-repairing rooms. As can be seen in this photograph, dated 1978, the wheat warehouse situated in the west end of the building is six-storeys high when the attic and basement are included. The four central floors were occupied by thirty large wheat silos, with a collective capacity of over 2,500 tonnes.

Grain would come in via the River Tyne, mainly imported from Canada, but also from the USA, Australia and Argentina. It would be processed at the mill and forty sacks of flour were produced each hour (or 5,600 sacks a week), with the finished product being dispatched by rail.

In 1908 the site was extended to include a soap works, with the Co-op sending workers from Manchester to fill key positions.

The chimney of the mill, which cannot be seen in this image, became a local landmark until the flour mill was demolished in 1980. (Archive photograph copyright Trevor Ermel)

A NEARBY STREET is named Flour Mill Road in recognition of the importance of the mill to Dunston. Houses now stand on the site of the former mill.

ESSOLDO CINEMA

IN SEPTEMBER 1904, plans were drawn up to construct an Alhambra Theatre of Varieties on the corner of High Street and Sunderland Road, named for the popular theatre and music hall in Leicester Square in the West End of London. However, it opened as the King's Theatre with a performance of the musical comedy *Floradora* on 9 October 1905. The 2,000-capacity theatre was designed by architect Stuart M. Mold with a Spanish Renaissance style exterior in red and white stone. It was built on a triangular site due to the sharp road junction of High Street and Sunderland Road.

By the end of November 1905, the owner was issued six summons as the theatre was putting on shows without a licence. Even once it was issued a licence, the theatre failed to attract the big stars as they preferred to work the main circuit theatres rather than those that were run independently. By 1907 the King's began screening short films as part of the variety programme.

The situation improved in 1915 when the theatre was taken over by Richard Thornton who owned a chain of variety theatres and brought better productions to the King's Theatre. The establishment was renamed as the Empire Theatre in 1918.

Films continued to make up part of the theatre's schedule and in October 1921 a projection box was built at the rear of the stage, with 'talkie' equipment being added in 1932.

In August 1946, the Empire Theatre was taken over by the Newcastle-based Essoldo cinema chain, and on 30 April 1950 it was renamed the Essoldo, with a heavier focus on screening feature-length films. The seating capacity was reduced to 1,087, as the gallery seating became redundant.

The Essoldo, seen here in the 1960s, screened the first 3D film in Gateshead in April 1953, and, the following year, it was the first to have CinemaScope installed. The last professional stage show was the Christmas pantomime *Jack and the Beanstalk* in 1965.

THE ESSOLDO CLOSED for the final time on 30 December 1967, and was demolished the following year along with many of the surrounding buildings to clear land for the building of a road viaduct. The office block, named Computer House, which can be seen in this present-day image, was built upon part of the site where the Essoldo once stood.

THE GATESHEAD DISPENSARY

IN DECEMBER 1831, Gateshead was hit by a cholera epidemic. It was the first time cholera had landed on British shores; brought to Britain when a ship carrying sailors who were infected with the disease had been allowed to dock in Sunderland in October of that year, despite instructions from the government that all ships coming from the Baltic states should be quarantined. Doctors were only too aware of what cholera did to the body, but they did not know how to stop the disease spreading, or how to treat the infected. Cholera took the lives of 234 Gateshead residents over a period of eleven months.

A dispensary to provide medical help to the poor was established at a public meeting
in 1832 by residents including the merchant William Brockett (who would go on to
become Mayor of Gateshead) and the Revd John Collinson. The first dispensary opened on
2 November 1832 on the High Street. In 1855, a building on the corner of Nelson Street and
West Street was bought to replace it and functioned as Gateshead's dispensary until 1946.

In this image of Nelson Street from the 1960s, the dispensary can be seen on the right
of the street. On the opposite side is Lloyds Bank. At the end of the street you can see the
shops at the bottom of West Street.

IN OCTOBER 1982 a plaque was erected at the Grade II listed building that was once
the dispensary in recognition of its historical importance to Gateshead. It reads:
'The Gateshead Dispensary 1832–1946. Founded after the outbreak of cholera in
1831 to assist in preserving the public health and make medicine available to the poor.
The Dispensary occupied this house 1855–1946.'

Today Nelson Street looks much the same, although the shops on West Street have
long since been demolished as Gateshead's road system has been improved. Lloyds
Bank remains, as does the dispensary building; however, it has recently been completely
refurbished and has become the headquarters for a national business travel company.

GIBSIDE HALL

GIBSIDE HALL WAS built by Sir William Blakiston between 1603 and 1620, on the site of a much older building. The hall was built within the country estate of Gibside, which had been acquired by the Blakiston family in 1540 through marriage.

In 1713, the Gibside estate changed hands, coming into the possession of the Bowes family, again due to marriage, with Sir William's great-granddaughter marrying Sir William Bowes of Streatlam Castle. The year 1767 saw Sir William Bowes' granddaughter, Mary, marry John Lyon, 9th Earl of Strathmore and Kinghorne. However, he was required to take the Bowes name as there was a clause in Mary's father's will to ensure that the Bowes lineage would be preserved should there be no male heir. The Bowes-Lyon family made a huge number of changes and improvements, including the landscaped gardens, Gibside chapel, the avenue of over 200 oaks with the chapel at one end, and the newly built Column of Liberty at the other. A banqueting hall was also built to entertain guests.

By the end of the nineteenth century, Gibside Hall was no longer the permanent residence of the Bowes-Lyon family, and, unmaintained, the building began its slow descent towards ruin.

In 1920 the family were forced to give up some of their magnificent residences and, as a result, anything of value was stripped from

Gibside Hall and moved to Glamis Castle in Angus, Scotland. In 1958, parts of Gibside Hall were demolished and the roof was removed, leaving the once-great mansion open to the elements and accelerating the decay.

ELIZABETH BOWES-LYON, better known by her title the Queen Mother, visited Gibside as a child. She returned in 1936 and several times during the 1960s, including attending a special service in which the restored Gibside Chapel and the avenue – also known as the Grand Walk – were entrusted to the National Trust.

The rest of the estate was sold off in separate lots during the 1970s, including the Grade II listed ruin of Gibside Hall, but the National Trust have since carefully reassembled Gibside and are restoring the estate to its former glory.

Sadly, it's too late to restore Gibside Hall and, as can be seen here, at present the hall has had to be fenced off as the building is unstable and could be dangerous. Work is underway to make the building safe so that visitors to Gibside may enter the hall once again.

HIGH STREET

GATESHEAD'S HIGH STREET is captured here in the early twentieth century, at which time it was said to be the longest high street in the country. Men in the dress of the time can be seen, as can some of the primary forms of transport for the people of Gateshead; including horse-drawn carts and the tramlines and overheard cables of the tram system, which until the electrification of the tram system in 1901 had been carriages pulled by steam locomotives.

The street provided anything that the locals could need in their day-to-day lives; including cobblers, ironmongers, butchers, hotels, theatres, a church and more than its fair share of pubs. Near to the tram terminus was the Half Moon pharmacy, which was vital for the people of Gateshead as there was only one doctor for every 2,500 people.

There were also early department stores such as Snowballs, which had been opened by William Snowball in 1850 and occupied Nos 15–21 High Street. It was the foremost store on the High Street and, in comparison to other department stores of the day, Snowballs was vast, employing over 200 people by the 1890s and extending back 400ft into Oakenwellgate.

In 1925, work began on the new Tyne Bridge, and this meant that the buildings at the bottom end of the High Street, nearest to the River Tyne, would have to be demolished to clear the land to construct an approach road to the bridge. This included the front section of Snowballs and so a new front section for the store was built 100ft back on Church Street, this was called Kent House.

TODAY KENT HOUSE, as can be seen here, is home to businesses including Raval restaurant and bar, Europcar car rental, Iris law firm, and Solution Group.

High Street is still the main shopping street of Gateshead, although it is almost unrecognisable from the High Street of over 100 years earlier; horse-drawn carts and trams have been replaced by cars, and a tarmacked road runs the length of the street.

HOLY CROSS CHURCH

THERE ARE RECORDS of a church in Ryton dating back to 1112. The current church is Holy Cross, pictured here in around 1900, and it is the oldest building in the village, being completed in around 1220.

It was built in an Early English style, on the bailey of a motte and bailey castle, which had been positioned here due to its excellent strategic position above the River Tyne.

In 1360 the upper tier of the tower was added, along with the octagonal spire built of oak and covered in lead that stands 120ft high and can be seen for miles around. The stained-glass windows were added in around 1450.

In 1886, a major refurbishment took place, which also saw an extension added to the building. A large organ chamber to house a fine Lewis organ was added as well as two vestries. The stunning east window created by Charles Eamer Kempe was also added, depicting the death, burial, resurrection and glorification of Christ.

TO CELEBRATE THE coming of the millennium, a ring of eight bells in a cast-iron frame, which would be called the Millennium Ring, was designed and installed by Fred Pembleton of Chesterfield in Derbyshire. The existing derelict bell chamber already housed four bells, so these were carefully removed and taken to Taylors of Loughborough, the largest working bell foundry in the world, to be retuned to ring perfectly with the four newly cast bells. These were installed by 11 December 1999 and rang in the new millennium.

Today the Grade I listed church has changed very little since the 1886 refurbishment, and lampposts and some of the table tombs in the churchyard have been awarded Grade II listed status.

IMPERIA CINEMA

THE IMPERIAL THEATRE opened in November 1910 on
Wellington Street in the centre of Felling, with a seating
capacity of 700. In July 1915, work began to increase the
capacity with the addition of a cantilevered dress circle,
this work was completed the following year. In 1923, it was
renamed the Imperia Cinema.

On 1 October 1929, the Imperia was devastated by
fire. The building was too damaged to be repaired and it
was demolished.

A year earlier, Joseph Smith had built the Palais de Dance
in Victoria Square on the former site of the Paragon Theatre,
which had been demolished back in 1905.

With a gap in the market for a cinema, work began to convert
the Palais de Dance for this purpose, with the circle having
seating for 210 and the ground floor seated a further 766.

On 25 August 1930, the New Imperia Cinema opened to
the people of Felling who referred to it as the 'Pally'. The film
showing on opening night was the new Janet Gaynor and
Charles Farrell musical *Sunny Side Up*.

In March 1932, a lounge opened in the cinema, which became popular as people could come and dance.

The Imperia was a popular place to go, but in February 1962 it closed with the final showing being Irwin Allen's *Voyage to the Bottom of the Sea*, starring Walter Pidgeon and Joan Fontaine.

It went on to become a bingo club, which it was by the time this photograph was taken in 1972. (Archive photograph copyright G. Hudson)

IN 1986 THE New Imperia Cinema was granted Grade II listed status by English Heritage.

In 2013, with the building having stood empty for three years, a £200,000 project was undertaken as part of a multi-million-pound redevelopment by the Felling Syndicate; restoring and refurbishing the building to its former glory, to be re-opened as the Imperia Bingo Club for the community of Felling to enjoy once again.

LOCKHAUGH VIADUCT

LOCKHAUGH VIADUCT, KNOWN locally as the 'Nine Arch Viaduct', was constructed in 1836, built completely of sandstone and carrying a single-track railway. It stands 80ft above a curve of the River Derwent and is 500ft long. It was built for the North East Railway and allowed the Derwent Valley Branch Railway to bypass Gibside Estate, because the Earl of Strathmore and Kinghorne would not allow the railway to pass through his land.

It is shown here being widened to accommodate a double track. This work commenced in 1905 and was completed in 1908.

THE DERWENT VALLEY Railway closed in 1962, and the viaduct now forms part of the Derwent Walk, offering unrivalled views for miles around. To the south-west, Gibside Estate is visible and the most prominent feature is the stunning statue of British Liberty in the grounds. Built between 1750 and 1759, the statue cost around £2,000. The Roman Doric column stands 140ft high and is topped by a 12ft figure holding the staff of maintenance and cap of liberty.

The viaduct is a popular vantage point for birdwatchers to watch for the Red Kites that Derwent Valley is famed for, following their successful reintroduction into the area in 2004.

METROCENTRE

THE WASTE GROUND upon which the Metrocentre was built was purchased for just £100,000 in the early 1970s.

Property developer and later Newcastle United owner Sir John Hall's company, Cameron Hall Developments, oversaw the construction, and it was financed by the Church Commissioners of England.

The centre opened in two phases, with the Red Mall opening on 28 April 1986 and the official opening on 14 October 1986. The Metrocentre, the original mega mall, the size of which had never been seen before, opened to great excitement and curiosity.

The House of Fraser, which acts as one of the many entrances into the Metrocentre and is across both floors of the Green Mall, is pictured here during its construction. (Archive photograph provided by Intu Metrocentre)

IN 1988, METROLAND opened at a cost of £20 million in the Yellow Mall; Europe's largest indoor amusement park included a roller coaster, pirate ship and ferris wheel. Metroland closed in 2008, despite strong local opposition and a petition including 4,000 signatures. The closure made way for a redevelopment of the Yellow Mall, which now includes a new Odeon Cinema with an IMAX screen.

Today the recently rebranded Intu Metrocentre has undertaken countless changes and improvements since it opened almost thirty years ago. Since it opened back in 1986, over half a billion shoppers have visited Europe's largest shopping centre and it now boasts over 340 stores populating the 1.9 million sq.ft of shopping and leisure space. Over 10,000 free car parking spaces, and excellent transport links, help attract over 2.5 million visitors to the Metrocentre each year.

MILLENNIUM BRIDGE

IN 1996, GATESHEAD launched a competition to design a bridge to complement the
existing six bridges that cross the River Tyne from Gateshead Quays on the south bank,
to the quayside of Newcastle upon Tyne on the north bank.

Gateshead residents voted for their favourite design from over 150 entries supplied
by leading architectural companies. The chosen design would go on to win Wilkinson
Eyre Architects and Gifford & Partners multiple awards. The design was for a pedestrian
and cycle bridge that would tilt 40° to allow small ships and boats to pass underneath.
It would even clean up its own litter as every time it opened anything lying on the deck of
the bridge would roll into special traps at each end.

This photograph shows the resulting Millennium Bridge, the world's first and only tilting bridge, being lifted into place in one piece on 20 November 2000 by Europe's largest floating crane: *Asian Hercules II.*

ON 28 JUNE 2001, 36,000 people lined the banks of the River Tyne to watch the completed Millennium Bridge tilt for the very first time; its appearance during this manoeuvre would quickly lead to it being nicknamed the 'Blinking Eye Bridge'. It officially opened for public crossing on 17 September 2001, and was dedicated by Queen Elizabeth II on 7 May 2002.

Despite the bridge being relatively new, it has quickly became a Gateshead landmark, even featuring on a first-class stamp and a £1 coin. Its grace and revolutionary engineering have attracted visitors to Gateshead from all over the world.

OAKENWELLGATE RECTORY

IT IS BELIEVED that this photograph may be the only surviving image of the former rectory of St Mary's church. Described in 1834 as a 'commodious house with gardens, and commands a fine view towards the river' it was, nevertheless, abandoned for a new rectory in Bensham in 1839. The western part of the old rectory was taken over by Susanna Stobart and became, in stark contrast to its previous purpose, a public house called the Brandling Arms, named for the interest in the Brandling Junction construction works and the company's contribution to the industrial development of Gateshead. In 1861 the Co-operative Society opened a store in the old rectory.

By the time this image was taken, in around 1886, industrial development had surrounded the building, as can be seen from the gasometer behind the building, and in the late 1880s the building was taken over by the North East Railway.

In around 1914 the building was mostly pulled down and was rebuilt as offices for the Judge Brand Co. Ltd.

TODAY, SAGE GATESHEAD stands on the site of the old rectory. Opened over the weekend of 17–19 December 2004, it is a centre for musical education, performance and conferences. Internally it consists of three separate performance spaces, insulated from one another to prevent sound and vibration travelling between them. Hall One is a 1,700-seat venue modelled on the Musikverein in Vienna and designed to be acoustically perfect. Hall Two is a unique ten-sided performance space with a seating capacity of 450, and the third building is a smaller rehearsal and performance hall.

The eye-catching curved glass and steel building is part of the Gateshead Quays development, which also includes the Millennium Bridge and the Baltic Centre for Contemporary Art.

OLD TOWN HALL

WHEN IT OPENED in February 1870, this was the third
building in Gateshead to be designated Gateshead's town hall.
Mayor Robert Stirling Newall had laid the foundation stone
two years earlier, on 11 June 1868, in a ceremony that ended
in tragedy. Thousands of the town's residents turned up for
the event and two special spectator platforms were erected
to accommodate the sizable crowd. However, one of these
platforms collapsed under the weight of 500 onlookers and
Mr Barnett, a 70 year old from Windmill Hills, lost his life.

From that day forth many superstitious Gateshead residents
feared the building might be cursed, and sadly more tragedy
would befall the beautiful building in the years that followed.
In 1935, the mayoress, Mrs Catherine White, collapsed and
died on the steps of the town hall, while in 1950 a lady's foot
was so badly trampled during the frenzied scramble for tickets
to that year's World Cup that it had to be amputated.

The town hall remained the centre of the town's government for over 100 years until the current civic centre opened in 1987.

ALTHOUGH THE TRAMLINES which can be seen running along West Street in the 1910 photograph have long gone, Gateshead's Old Town Hall, as it has become known, has changed very little since it first opened almost 150 years ago.

It had been used as office space for the council for decades, until the interior and exterior were refurbished and Sage Gateshead took over the management of the Grade II listed building at the suggestion of Gateshead Council. In January 2014, the Old Town Hall was opened as an intimate venue for performance and the arts, as well as being a stunning location in which to host conferences, events and weddings.

THE PHOENIX

CURLEYS ON THE High Street began life as the Phoenix. The earliest-recorded landlady was Jane Hindmarsh, who held the licence for the public house back in 1841 when she was aged 60. By 1873 it was in the ownership of a J. Lamb; however, it would be the subsequent owner who would really become synonymous with the popular watering hole. His name was Will Cawley but he was much better known as Will Curley.

Will Cawley was a boxer who fought American Patsy Haley in 1897 at Gateshead's Standard Theatre for the world 118lb title when Will was just 19. He went on to win comfortably and this would be the first of many titles he attained during his career. He became known as Will Curley when the boxing press misunderstood his Gateshead accent and began calling him Curley; the name stuck.

By the time Will retired from boxing he was running the Phoenix. It was nicknamed 'Curleys' by the locals until his death in 1937. Will's son, Robert, took over the running of the bar following his father's passing until 1964 when Scottish & Newcastle Breweries bought the bar.

In this photograph, taken in 1971, the pub is still named the Phoenix but bears the name of Will Curley above the door. In the years that followed it was officially renamed Curleys in the honour of its most famous landlord.

TODAY CURLEYS HASN'T changed much, the newer name of the bar can clearly be seen on the modern signage and it has had a makeover, with the dark paint of the 1971 photograph replaced with a much lighter paint job. The main change is that the building next door has been demolished, leaving Curleys standing alone on the corner of the High Street.

REDHEUGH PARK

GATESHEAD AFC STARTED life as South Shields FC but, struggling both on and off the field, the dramatic decision was made in 1930 to move the club to another town in the hope of obtaining more support. Newcastle upon Tyne was considered but Gateshead was decided upon due to the enthusiasm showed by Gateshead Council towards the venture.

Gateshead AFC was born and the search began for a suitable ground for the new club to call home. Sites at Low Fell and Sheriff Hill were considered before a site in the Teams area of Gateshead was chosen, on land which had been a worked-out clay pit.

On 30 August 1930, the new ground, named Redheugh Park, was officially opened and 15,545 spectators turned up to watch Gateshead AFC play their first ever Football League game, winning 2–1 against Doncaster Rovers.

In 1960, the club lost Football League status and further relegations, and financial troubles blighted the side and Redheugh Park for the next decade.

By 1971, when this photograph was taken, Redheugh Park was run down and, in the 1971/72 season, there was a fire at the ground. With no money to repair the ground, this was the end for Redheugh Park and the club was forced to move to the Gateshead Youth Stadium on the A184 Felling Bypass.

In 1972, Redheugh Park was falling apart, infested with weeds and had dilapidated stands. It was demolished soon after.

Gateshead AFC were fairing no better at their new home and, in August 1973, having resigned from the Midland League, they went into liquidation.

ALTERNATIVE GATESHEAD TEAMS came and went over the next four years and in 1977 Gateshead were resurrected as Gateshead FC. The club joined the Northern Premier League and returned to the Youth Stadium, which by now had been upgraded and renamed as Gateshead International Stadium, is pictured here in the present day.

The club has gone from strength to strength in the years that have followed, and in the 2013/14 season they made it to the Conference Premier play-off final at Wembley. The winner of the game would join the Football League; however, Gateshead lost a close game 2–1 to Cambridge United.

Plans for a new 7,856-capacity stadium for the club were unveiled in October 2009, to be built in the town centre opposite the Gateshead Civic Centre on the site of the former North Durham Cricket & Rugby Club. These plans have since been shelved, but Chairman Graham Wood has hopes that this stadium will eventually be built to take the club forward.

The land that Redheugh Park once stood on was left unused for almost twenty years following its demolition in 1972, with the outline of the stadium being visible as humps in the grassland. In 1990 the land was levelled and used as a car park, and in the mid-1990s the Pitz five-a-side soccer centre was built on the site of the old football stadium. This has since been renamed Power League.

SALTMEADOWS

THIS IMAGE SHOWS the Saltmeadows area, situated to the south of Gateshead town centre, on the southern shore of the River Tyne and the Newcastle Quayside on the opposite bank. Local men and a group of boys are walking along the mud flats, a popular summertime pastime in years long gone for the people of the area.

In the nineteenth century, when Britain was famously considered to be 'the workshop of the world', Saltmeadows was a busy industrial area that was home to industries including iron manufacturing, rope making, chemical and soap manufacture, brick making, shipbuilding, and working several coalmines, with the area boasting the first coal staithe in all of Tyneside, dating back to the seventeenth century. The skyline along the Tyne was dominated by smoking chimneys and the shoreline held boats as far as the eye could see.

By the beginning of the twentieth century, engineering works became one of Saltmeadows primary industries, taking the place of the iron manufacturers that was very much an industry in decline.

New industries came to Saltmeadows by the 1930s, including the North East Electricity Supply Company and Northumberland Press. It was also during the 1930s that the area was considered as the location of a new trading estate; however, a site in the Team Valley was chosen instead and would be built as the Team Valley Trading Estate.

SALTMEADOWS REMAINS AN industrial and commercial area. The stretch along the shoreline was a popular picnic destination and cycle path by the end of the twentieth century. However, in 2005, soil samples taken at Saltmeadows showed the area to be heavily contaminated with dioxins and Gateshead Council closed the area to the public.

In 2009, after a £2 million scheme to make the area safe to the public, Saltmeadows was reopened for the people of Gateshead by Councillor Michael McNestry, the Cabinet member responsible for the environment, and children from nearby Bill Quay Primary School.

It can be seen here in this modern photograph. To the left of the image, Gateshead's unique Kittiwake Tower is visible, it is the UK's only aerial Local Nature Reserve and provides a home to around 100 nesting pairs of Kittiwakes.

SALTWELL PARK

SALTWELL PARK WAS created on the 37-acre Saltwellside Estate that Gateshead Council purchased in 1875 for £35,000 from William Wailes. A leading exponent of stained glass, Wailes lived in a grand Victorian mansion called Saltwell Towers in the centre of the estate. The council rented Saltwell Towers back to Wailes until he passed away in 1881.

The park was planned out by landscape-designer Edward Kemp and became known informally as 'The People's Park', a nickname that is commonly used to this day. There was no officially opening ceremony but the park was used by the people of Gateshead from late 1876.

Saltwell Park Lake can be seen here, and it was part of Kemp's plans for the park; however, it was not added until four years after the park opened. It was designed for the purpose of boating and skating, and in 1886 the lake was first used for model boating, which has been a fixture of the lake ever since. In 1909 the island in the centre of the lake was home to a bandstand. This meant that musicians were required to travel across to the island by rowing boats with their instruments. In 1921, following the expansion of the park to 55 acres, a bandstand was constructed in the new area of parkland, to the relief of the musicians who played at Saltwell Park.

SALTWELL PARK AND the surrounding area have changed hugely since the park first opened for the people of the town. By the end of the twentieth century the park had been neglected and fell into disrepair. However, between 1999 and 2005 a restoration project costing £9.6 million returned the park to its Victorian splendour and now it is visited by over 2 million people each year.

In 2005, Saltwell Park was named 'Britain's Best Park', and the following year it was chosen as the Civic Trust Park of the Year. Every year since 2006 it has won a Green Flag Award, and in 2013 it was listed as one of fifty-five Green Heritage sites in the UK.

BOER WAR MEMORIAL, SALTWELL PARK

IN THE CENTRAL section of Saltwell Park, around 100m south of the Victorian mansion of Saltwell Towers, is one of three war memorials found within the park. Added in 1905, it is a bronze angel holding aloft a laurel crown, atop a granite plinth that commemorates the men of Gateshead who lost their life fighting in the Second Boer War (1899–1902).

In was unveiled on 11 November 1905, a day which coincidentally would become Armistice Day from 1918 onwards, and is inscribed: 'In Grateful Remembrance of the Gateshead Men who lost their lives in their Country's Service. This Memorial was erected by their fellow Townsmen, October 1905.'

The roll of honour contains the names of seventy-six brave Gateshead men, and is a stark reminder of the impact that the war had on the town.

THE PRESENT-DAY image shows how little the memorial and the area of Saltwell Park that surrounds it has changed. One of the changes that can be seen, however, is the wooden bridge visible in the newer image. This is another of Saltwell Park's war memorials; this timber footbridge is 12ft wide, 22ft long and named the Primosole Bridge. It was built in 2002 in tribute to the men of the Durham Light Infantry who died whilst crossing the original Primosole Bridge in Sicily during an Allied invasion of the Second World War named Operation Fustian. This memorial was added during the Lottery-funded restoration of the park that took place between 1999–2005, and is a newer copy of an original Edwardian tribute that used to cross the ha-ha.

SALTWELL TOWERS

SALTWELL TOWERS, ORIGINALLY named Saltwell Park House, was built in 1862 in the centre of a 37-acre estate owned by William Wailes, a leading craftsman in the field of stained glass. Its appearance, as can be seen in this photograph from the early twentieth century, is an eclectic mix of Gothic and Elizabethan, and the exterior is dominated by great asymmetrical towers, tall chimneystacks and a multitude of parapets. It is built of dark brick with patterns of yellow brickwork.

In 1875, William Wailes sold the estate and his family home of Saltwell Towers to Gateshead Council who were searching for a suitable site for a park for the people of Gateshead. In 1884, Saltwell Towers was bought by Joseph Shipley who lived there from 1884 until his death in 1909. His enormous art collection and a generous

donation left in his will saw the Shipley Art Gallery built on Prince Consort Road.

During the First World War the building was used as a hospital, and after the war ended in 1918 it was left empty until it became an industrial museum from 1933 until 1968.

From 1968, the building, much like Saltwell Park around it, fell into disrepair. Dry rot set in and the once-great mansion of Saltwell Towers became a roofless, derelict shell, with only three external walls standing.

IN 1999 A £9.6 million restoration project began to transform both Saltwell Towers – the building that had formed the very heart of the park for over 150 years – and Saltwell Park.

On Wednesday, 14 July 2004, Saltwell Towers was reopened, with William Wailes' great-great-grandson Peter Rankine Defty and his daughter in attendance as special guests at the official opening.

The mansion has been turned into the visitor centre for the park and includes a cafe, IT facilities and an exhibition on the fascinating history of the Saltwell Park and Towers.

In 2005 the Society of Chief Architects of Local Authorities (SCALA) awarded the restored Saltwell Towers its Civic Building of the Year.

SCOTSWOOD CHAIN BRIDGE

CAPTURED HERE IN around 1910, the Old Scotswood Bridge – or the 'Chain Bridge' as it was known locally – was a suspension toll bridge over the River Tyne, linking the west end of Newcastle on the north bank of the river with Blaydon on the south bank. It had two stone towers from which the deck, which formed the road, was suspended by wrought-iron chains. Construction began in 1829 to the designs of John Green, and it opened on 16 April 1831 to great excitement of the locals and a grand opening ceremony. Dignitaries formed a procession from the Assembly Rooms at Newcastle, along the Scotswood Road and over the new bridge into Blaydon, on to Swalwell, and back over the bridge into Newcastle.

In 1905 the bridge was bought by the Newcastle Corporation, and by 1907 there was no longer a toll to cross.

In 1931 the bridge had to be strengthened, with the chains changed to stronger steel wire ropes, and the decking itself strengthened. This allowed the weight limit to be raised from 6 tonnes to 10 tonnes. The bridge was also widened from 17ft to 19.5ft and two footpaths were added.

In 1941 it was suggested that, despite the 1931 improvements, the existing Scotswood Bridge was too narrow for modern vehicles, and the repair costs had become unfeasible. Almost twenty years later, in 1960, permission was granted to demolish the bridge and build a replacement.

A new bridge was designed by Mott, Hay and Anderson, and construction commenced 92m west of the existing bridge on 18 September 1964. It was built by a consortium of Mitchell Construction and Kinnear Moody Group Ltd, and the steelwork was erected by Dorman Long. The existing bridge continued to operate during the construction of its replacement.

THE NEW BRIDGE was opened on 20 March 1967. Built to a new box girder design, this new bridge wasn't without its problems, having to undergo almost £500,000 worth of improvements to strengthen it in 1971, only four years after it opened. Further work was carried out in 1979/80, again in 1983, and it was closed completely for several months in 1990.

SHIPLEY ART GALLERY

THE SHIPLEY ART Gallery opened on 29 November 1917. This was
only made possible due to a bequest from a wealthy solicitor and
art collector, Joseph Shipley, who had passed away in 1909. Shipley,
a very wealthy man, had lived at Saltwell Park House – now named
Saltwell Towers – from 1884 until his death. He had amassed a
collection of 2,500 paintings; a collection that it is reported he started
when he bought his first painting at the age of just 16.

On his death, Shipley donated a large amount of money to
charity, as well as leaving all of his paintings to the City of Newcastle
along with £30,000 with which to create a gallery to house them.
He specifically excluded the Laing Art Gallery from this as he
considered it too small. After three years of debate and discussion,
Newcastle rejected this bequest, and the offer was passed on to,
and accepted by, Gateshead Municipal Council.

It was decided that it would be impossible to build a gallery that
could display the entirety of Shipley's collection, so the executors
recommended 359 oil paintings and watercolours, a further 145 were

selected by the Gateshead Committee, and the remaining paintings were sold. The 504 selected paintings would make up the gallery's initial permanent collection and would be named the *Shipley Bequest*.

Work began on a new gallery at the south end of Prince Consort Road, designed by Arthur Stockwell of Newcastle. The building was built in a Neoclassical style and the front was of stone with a Doric-columned portico roof. Two seated figures are surmounted atop these, one representing the arts and one representing science.

TODAY THE GALLERY has changed little, although the collection within has continued to grow and now numbers over 10,000 items, including William C. Irving's spectacular painting, *The Blaydon Races*. Over the last twenty-five years, the gallery has become established as a national centre for contemporary craft and has built up one of the best collections outside of London, with over 700 pieces by the country's leading craft makers, including jewelry, textiles, metalwork, glass, studio ceramics and furniture.

Impossible to ignore in either photograph is the magnificent monument in the foreground. Built in 1921, this is one of the region's most ambitious memorials and stands in honour of Gateshead men who lost their lives during the First World War. The roll of honour, which once appeared on the monument, has been moved to the nearby Central Library for safekeeping.

ST ANDREW'S CHURCH

ST ANDREW'S CHURCH is located in Lamesley, only a few hundred metres from the A1, in the base of the Team Valley. The church once served the community that grew around it; however, there is no longer a village close the church and St Andrew's stands alone except for the church hall, formerly a school, to the north.

The church is a neat stone structure in the Early English style. It dates back to 1286; however, it was so extensively rebuilt in 1758 that nothing visible remains from the previous building. Church registers exist from as far back as 1603 and the church font is from 1664.

In 1821 the church was extended. Further improvements were made in 1847 when £1,600 was spent rebuilding the chancel, and in 1884 further restoration was made costing £1,400.

The church is pictured here in 1921, viewed from the west. The tower rises in three stages and the clock that can be seen was added in 1904 to commemorate the 3rd Earl of Ravensworth. A panel is inscribed, 'To the glory of God and in memory of Athole 3rd Earl of Ravensworth. Born 6th August 1833 died 7th February 1904. The clock in this tower was placed by his widow.'

THE CHURCH HAS changed very little externally, as can be seen when comparing the earlier photograph to this present-day image. The original photograph was taken from within a field opposite the church, but the same view is no longer possible due to the dense trees lining the field today.

ST CHAD'S CHURCH

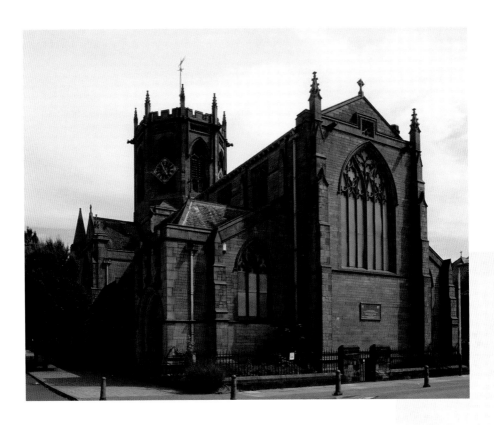

THE BUILDING OF the Anglican church of St Chad in Bensham was completed in 1903, to the design of architect William Searle Hicks, who died in 1902 before seeing his vision for the church realised. The costs for the building of the church were met by founder Emily Matilda Easton of Nest House in Felling, who had amassed great wealth from the coal industry; the Oakwellgate Colliery in Gateshead, amongst others, was owned by her brothers James and Thomas Easton.

St Chad was a native of Northumberland in the seventh century. Along with his brother Cedd, he was a pupil of St Aidan on the Holy Island of Lindisfarne and would go on to become abbot of several monasteries, Bishop of the Northumbrians, and then Bishop of Mercia. He would later become a saint. He is credited, alongside Cedd, with bringing Christianity to the Kingdom of Mercia.

St Chad's church was consecrated on 29 September 1903, and Miss Easton's nephew presented the petition on behalf of his elderly aunt. There were many notable members of the community in attendance,

including eighty members of the clergy, the Mayor of Gateshead and the bishops of Durham and Newcastle.

The church's pulpit has elaborate carvings of famous stories from the Bible, and a statue of the church's patron saint, St Chad. The lectern is a pelican, which may seem unusual in a church, however, it's an ancient Christian symbol of sacrifice and Durham Cathedral has a similar lectern.

The north window, added around 1915 by stained-glass artist Leonard Walker, is a memorial to Emily Easton and the Embleton family. It is reputed to be the only example of Walker's stained glass in the North of England and contains scenes of the Ascension in the Arts and Crafts style. A portrait of Emily Easton also hangs in the church.

The east and west windows are by the Percy Bacon Brothers, and the west window is in memory of the architect, William Searle Hicks.

AS CAN BE seen in this early postcard and present-day comparison photograph, the church has barely changed externally in the 111 years since St Chad's first opened its doors to the people of Bensham.

ST EDMUND'S CHAPEL

ST EDMUND'S CHAPEL, situated on Gateshead High Street, is one of Gateshead's oldest buildings. It was originally built on a site known as 'Gateshead Head' in around 1247, as the Hospital of St Edmund, Bishop and Confessor, 'for the spiritual refreshment of the soul'.

In 1594, John Ingram, a young Jesuit priest, was executed outside the building on account of his religious beliefs. A stone cross was erected to commemorate the scene, as well as marking the head of the town of Gateshead.

Following the Dissolution of the Monasteries, the building fell into disrepair. In 1837, the roofless building was restored, with famed Newcastle architect John Dobson overseeing the work. There had been another St Edmund's Chapel built on the old Durham Road elsewhere in the town, so the building was reopened as Trinity Chapel.

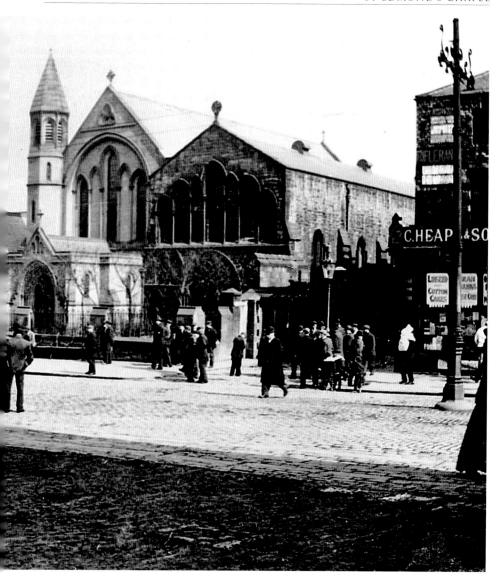

In 1893, the year before this photograph was taken, the building was extended and changed its name once again to Holy Trinity church. The building closed in 1969 and, with the other St Edmund's long since demolished, it reopened in 1980 as St Edmund's Chapel, the parish church of Gateshead. The 1893 extension, seen to the left of the building, would become a community centre.

SINCE 2010 THE church has also been the venue for Sanctuary Artspace, a gallery installed along the north wall of the building with exhibitions held almost every week of the year. A banner, which can be seen in this photograph on the railings outside, reads: 'Sanctuary Artspace. Gateshead's newest gallery in Gateshead's oldest building.'

ST HELEN'S CHURCH

THE FOUNDATION STONE of St Helen's church in Low Fell, pictured here in 1900, was laid on 29 October 1873 and the church was consecrated on 29 August 1876. The cost of construction was £13,000 and was paid for by coal mining magnate Edward Joicey of the nearby Whinney House. The result was a beautiful Victorian stone church, built in the Early English style, with an open timbered roof, cruciform in plan.

The church organ is particularly fine; it cost £1,000 and was made by Father Henry Willis, notable organ builder.

The windows of the church are lancet-type and, although the makers of some of the stained-glass windows are unknown, those that are attributable include the work of

respected stained-glass artists Sir Edward Coley Burne-Jones, George Joseph Baguley and Charles Earner Kempe.

To encourage his colliery workers to attend church, Edward Joicey built a bridge over Whinney Dene on his estate to make it easier for them to reach the service.

The church could originally seat 500 but the number is now around 330 due to alterations and redesigns that have taken place since it first opened.

The Father Willis organ was rebuilt in 1949 by H. Vincent of Sunderland.

ST HELEN'S IS now a Grade II listed building. It remains very much as it was built in 1876, and is still popular with the parishioners of Low Fell. The vantage point of the original photograph is no longer possible due to the houses that have since been built around the church. A high tree line also surrounds it, practically hiding the church from the road that passes it, with the exception of the spire, which can still be seen for miles around.

ST JOHN'S CHURCH

IN 1809 A decision was made that a church should be built upon Gateshead Fell, with a grant of £1,000 awarded by the Church Building Commission and an acre of land allocated for this new structure.

On 13 May 1824, the foundation stone was laid by Revd John Collinson. The coinage of the reigning monarch, from a penny through to a sovereign, were placed inside a flint-glass bottle placed inside a cavity within the foundation stone, alongside a silver tablet bearing an inscription of the date and those who performed the ceremony: the dignitaries in attendance, the reverend, the trustees, and the architect. The building was completed the following year to the designs of architect John Ions, and consecrated on 30 August. The total cost of the newly opened St John's church was £2,742. The church's first rector, Revd William Hawks, was inducted the following month. The church stands over 500ft above sea level, and the spire is the highest point in all of Gateshead.

When this photograph was taken in 1900, the rector was Revd Johnathan Mitchell.

On 26 April 1950, the church was officially listed as a building of special architectural and historical interest, and was awarded Grade II listed status.

EXTERNALLY TODAY, THE building looks almost identical, despite the 114-year gap between the photographs being taken. It's no longer possible to capture the church from the same vantage point as the original due to the houses that have been built around the church in the intervening years.

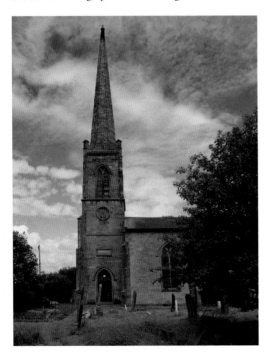

Internally, the church has undergone major changes in recent years. Long-awaited building work commenced in 1998 to build two meeting rooms, toilets and a kitchen. A Harrison & Harrison organ was salvaged from the disused St Aiden's church in Consett. The church pews were removed and replaced with modern seating and the floors carpeted. This has brought St John's church into the twenty-first century, and not only made it a more pleasant venue for church services delivered by the current rector, Revd Andrew West, but also allowed for midweek activities, with the space being used for community purposes.

ST JOSEPH'S CATHOLIC CHURCH

THE VENERABLE BEDE wrote of a monastery in 'Getehed' in the seventh century, which served the Catholics of the town. After the Dissolution of the Monasteries, the estate came into the possession of the Riddell family.

In the chapel of the estate, Mass continued to be held – in secrecy – until 1746, when the chapel, along with the Riddell mansion, was sacked and burnt to the ground.

For over 100 years, Gateshead was without a Catholic church, until plans were made in 1850 by William Hogarth, Bishop of Hexham and Newcastle, to start a parish to be

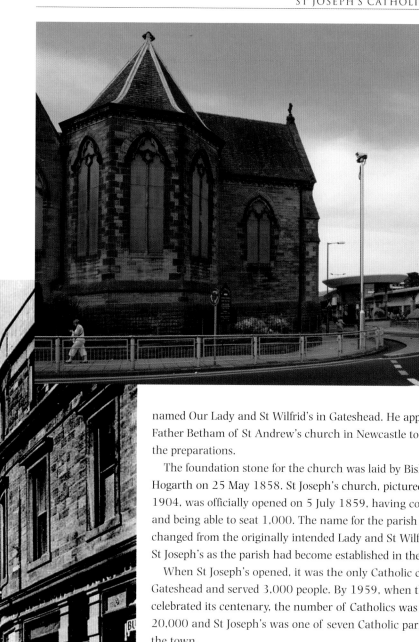

named Our Lady and St Wilfrid's in Gateshead. He appointed
Father Betham of St Andrew's church in Newcastle to make
the preparations.

The foundation stone for the church was laid by Bishop
Hogarth on 25 May 1858. St Joseph's church, pictured here in
1904, was officially opened on 5 July 1859, having cost £3,000
and being able to seat 1,000. The name for the parish had
changed from the originally intended Lady and St Wilfrid's to
St Joseph's as the parish had become established in the town.

When St Joseph's opened, it was the only Catholic church in
Gateshead and served 3,000 people. By 1959, when the church
celebrated its centenary, the number of Catholics was around
20,000 and St Joseph's was one of seven Catholic parishes in
the town.

THE CHURCH TODAY has changed very little, while the streets
and buildings that surround it have changed drastically. The street
that can be seen opposite the church in the 1904 photograph
was demolished to make way for the Gateshead Interchange,
a transport interchange that opened in 1985 to serve the Tyne
and Wear Metro system and local bus services.

ST MARY'S CHURCH.

PICTURED HERE IN around 1960, St Mary's church, a riverside landmark high above the River Tyne, was the only Anglican church in the town until St John's was built in 1825 at Sheriff Hill. This led to it being considered the 'mother church' of Gateshead and it was the only place where marriages could take place. It is unknown when the church was originally built, although historians suggest the building dates back to the 1100s, built upon the site of a previous church that was destroyed by fire in 1080. A local historian has speculated that some of the oldest stones resemble the Roman style and could have been reclaimed from the remains of a nearby Roman building.

Despite being a place of worship, the ancient building has endured a stormy history. During the English Civil War, Parliamentarian soldiers were stationed at the church's rectory. The rectory was destroyed and the church was damaged by cannon balls. In the Great Fire of 1854, the church was damaged by fire. By 1979, the building, having ceased to be used as a church, was once more ablaze; this time fire consumed the building and it was largely destroyed. It was rebuilt to be used as an auction room, but in 1983 the building was once again damaged by fire.

IN THE PHOTOGRAPH taken today, the church does not appear to have changed from the 1960s image, although the Tyne Bridge to the left of the image has now been largely obscured by the trees which can be seen, albeit much smaller, in the original. It is internally that the big changes have taken place. In a £1.2 million project funded by Gateshead Council, the European Regional Development Fund and the Heritage Lottery Fund, the interior of the Grade I listed church was stripped out and it reopened on 16 December 2008 as St Mary's Heritage Centre; a unique visitor attraction in a stunning location on the Gateshead Quay, with libraries, art and local heritage all incorporated in a single venue.

TEAM VALLEY TRADING ESTATE

IN THE 1930s, the local government decided to invest around £2 million in establishing the Team Valley Trading Estate. On 27 July 1936, surveying of the Team Valley site began, with the survey party working long hours, seven days a week for eight weeks.

In October of the same year, G. Wimpey & Co. was awarded the contract for the development with an initial contract sum of £80,000 and the agreement that the first factory would be ready within a year. Many local men were employed as labourers on the project.

Progress was swift and this photograph, taken in 1937, shows the Team Valley under construction. The 'Kingsway' can be seen, a wide central artery, almost 2 miles long.

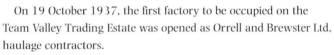

On 19 October 1937, the first factory to be occupied on the Team Valley Trading Estate was opened as Orrell and Brewster Ltd, haulage contractors.

On 22 February 1939, King George VI and Queen Elizabeth formally opened the Team Valley Trading Estate, which included a central headquarters (now used by English Partnerships), a post office, a bank and industrial buildings as well as some smaller industrial units for start-up ventures. The southern end was the location of the National Coal Board's regional headquarters. The royal visitors spent three hours inspecting the new trading estate and unveiled a commemorative plaque at St George's House, attended by 500 people.

In the years that followed, the Team Valley Trading Estate was described as 'the greatest achievement of industrial planning Europe has ever seen'.

TODAY, TEAM VALLEY is recognised worldwide, and is one of the largest industrial estates in Britain with a land bank in excess of 50 acres hosting over 700 businesses, which employ over 20,000 people.

Many changes have taken place since the estate opened all those years ago. The Team Valley Retail Park takes up a very small section of the estate but is very popular. The site on which the National Coal Board's Regional Headquarters once stood is now a Sainsbury's supermarket. In the last decade the development of Maingate, at the northern end of the estate, has provided a number of service facilities, including a hotel, a gym, shops, food outlets and serviced offices.

THE METROPOLE
THEATRE

THE METROPOLE THEATRE, situated on the corner of High Street and Jackson Street, opened on 28 September 1896 to a production of William Barrett's play *The Sign of the Cross*. It was the largest theatre in all of Gateshead, seating 2,500 people, and it was also the most luxurious. It had a fine marble staircase with brass handrails and an elaborately decorated auditorium ceiling depicting angels arranging garlands. The plays were provided by touring companies and initially proved a huge hit. However, by 1919 the touring production companies had declined in number and the building was converted to

a cinema, later renamed the Scala Cinema. The Scala was the first cinema in England to use rear projection, and a large orchestra played the music to accompany the silent films until a Cinema Organ was fitted at the cost of £3,000.

The Scala Cinema closed in 1956, the year after this photograph was taken, and in 1960 the cinema was demolished, although the Metropole Hotel, which formed part of the building, was spared.

TODAY THE METROPOLE Hotel is now a public house called the Metropole, and has changed little when compared to the 1955 photograph.

Upon the site of the once-grand Metropole Theatre (which then became Scala Cinema) is now a TSB bank, built in a style typical of the 1960s.

TRINITY SQUARE

CAPTURED HERE IN the 1970s, Trinity Square was a shopping centre and multi-storey car park that dominated the skyline of Gateshead ever since it was opened in 1967. It was noted for the Brutalist design that was considered cutting-edge architecture in 1962 when it was designed by Rodney Gordon of the Owen Luder Partnership. However, by the time it opened five years later, it was considered unattractive with poor access, and was made of concrete that weathered poorly.

The car park featured prominently in the 1971 Michael Caine film *Get Carter* so became known as the '*Get Carter* Car Park'.

The Gateshead Interchange opened in 1985, offering excellent bus and metro links. This service, combined with the development of the Metrocentre and the shopping on offer on Newcastle's Northumberland Street (including the Eldon Square Shopping Centre), meant that the car park at Trinity Square became largely redundant. In 1995 the worsening conditioning of the structure led to the upper floors of the car park having to be closed. The future looked bleak for the '*Get Carter* Car Park' and, in June 2007, despite strong opposition calling for it to be preserved as a Gateshead landmark, it was confirmed that Trinity Square would be demolished and rebuilt as a new town centre shopping complex.

IN MARCH 2013, the £150 million Trinity Square opened, boasting a seven-screen cinema complex, a Tesco Extra store and 240,000sq.ft of retail and leisure space including shops such as Boots and Sports Direct, and bars and restaurants including Nandos.

It is pictured here in the summer of 2014, with over 3 million visitors coming to Trinity Square since it opened a little over a year earlier. The *Halo* sculpture that can be seen was added in February 2014, and the stainless-steel structure created by North East artist Steve Newby is the largest of its type in the world.

VICTORIA ROAD METHODIST CHURCH

THE METHODIST CHURCH has had a presence in the Teams area of Gateshead since the first Wesleyan chapel in Low Teams opened in 1856 to serve an area becoming increasingly overtaken by industrial development. The Ordnance Survey map of 1897 shows two Wesleyan chapels in the Teams, but the names of these, when they opened and when they closed, has been lost to time.

The Methodist church and adjoining Sunday school on Victoria Road were built in 1882, and served an area stretching from the centre of Gateshead to Crawcrook along the Tyne Valley.

During the Second World War, the church did its bit for the war effort, acting as an emergency feeding centre.

In 1968, three years before this photograph was taken, some routine maintenance work was being carried out when the ceiling collapsed, falling into the building. Some 2 tonnes of beams, plaster and cement crashed down around the builder yet he miraculously survived with only a broken arm and a few bumps and bruises. During the rebuild, a few modern touches were made to the church, including the addition of a meeting room.

IN 1983 THE church was again struck by disaster when gale-force winds battered the church, bringing down a gable wall, with over 300 bricks falling into the church and damage caused to the church's organ. A burst water main struck in 1987, causing further damage. Water was forced over 35ft into the air and flooded not only the church, but also the surrounding streets.

The church is now closed down, left empty and unused, and faces an uncertain future. As can be seen in this present-day photograph, it is up for sale, offering a development opportunity to the buyer.

WHINNEY HOUSE

THE LAND UPON which Whinney House was built was bought in 1864 by two brothers, wealthy coal owners John and Edward Joicey. Work began on a mansion, and when it was completed in 1867, Whinney House was the largest mansion in Low Fell. It stood in huge grounds that included an enormous dene.

Later that year the house became the sole possession of Edward Joicey, as John handed over his share of Whinney House to his brother as a gift. Edward and his family lived in the house, happily enjoying life in Low Fell. When the village's church, St Helen's, was built in 1876, Edward generously met the £13,000 construction costs.

Edward passed away in 1879 and his widow Eleanor continued to live in Whinney House until her death in 1906.

The trustees of the estate let it out to a colliery owner from Morpeth, a Mr Fraser, who lived there at the time this photograph was taken in 1910. In 1913 it changed hands again and became a Catholic retreat, offering local workers the opportunity to spend three days meditating and reflecting on matters of a spiritual nature.

With the outbreak of the First World War there was a need for hospitals to treat those injured in battle, and in 1915 Whinney House became a temporary hospital.

In 1921 the building was purchased by the Gateshead Corporation and used as a hospital to treat sufferers of tuberculosis, before later becoming a home for the elderly.

IN MORE RECENT years it was a centre for people with learning difficulties, before being converted into Gateshead Jewish College.

In 2012 the Grade II listed building was put up for sale with an asking price of £420,000. It was purchased by developers and this 2014 image shows Whinney House being converted into two- and three-bedroom luxury apartments.

If you enjoyed this book, you may also be interested in…

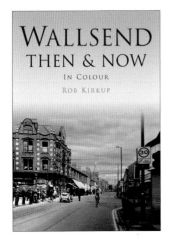

Wallsend Then & Now
ROB KIRKUP

Wallsend has a rich heritage, which is uniquely reflected in this delightful, full-colour compilation. Contrasting a selection of forty-five archive images alongside modern photographs taken from the same location, this new book reveals the changing faces, buildings and streets of Wallsend during the last century. Comparing the workers of yesteryear with today's tradespeople, along with some famous landmarks and little-known street scenes, this is a wide-ranging look at the area's absorbing history.

978 0 7524 6561 6

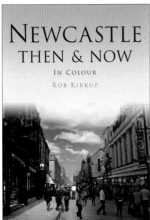

Newcastle Then & Now
ROB KIRKUP

The changing face of Newcastle is revealed through unique archive images of yesteryear alongside modern photographs of the city today. This full-colour collection will provide visitors with a glimpse of how the city used to be, in addition to awakening nostalgic memories for those who live or work here.

978 0 7524 6566 1

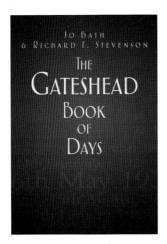

The Gateshead Book of Days
JO BATH & RICHARD F. STEVENSON

Taking you through the year day by day, *The Gateshead Book of Days* contains quirky, eccentric, shocking, amusing and important events and facts from different periods in the history of the town. Ideal for dipping into, this addictive little book will keep you entertained and informed. Featuring hundreds of snippets of information gleaned from the vaults of Gateshead's archives and covering the social, criminal, political, religious, agricultural, industrial and sporting history of the region, it will delight residents and visitors alike.

978 0 7524 6867 9

Visit our website and discover thousands of other History Press books.

www.thehistorypress.co.uk